Octopuses

by Lola M. Schaefer

Consulting Editor: Gail Saunders-Smith, Ph.D.

Consultant: Jody Byrum, Science Writer,
SeaWorld Education Department

Pebble Books

an imprint of Capstone Press
Mankato, Minnesota

Pebble Books are published by Capstone Press
151 Good Counsel Drive, P.O. Box 669, Mankato, Minnesota 56002
http://www.capstone-press.com

2 3 4 5 6 7 07 06 05 04 03 02

Library of Congress Cataloging-in-Publication Data
Schaefer, Lola M., 1959–
    Octopuses / by Lola M. Schaefer.
    p. cm.—(Ocean life)
    Summary: Simple text and photographs introduce octopuses and their behavior.
    ISBN 0-7368-0246-0 (hardcover)
    ISBN 0-7368-8217-0 (paperback)
    1. Octopus—Juvenile literature. [1. Octopus.] I. Title. II. Series: Schaefer,
Lola M. 1950– Ocean life.
QL430.3.O2S32
594'.56—dc21   98-31444

Note to Parents and Teachers

The Ocean Life series supports national science standards for units
on the diversity and unity of life. The series shows that animals
have features that help them live in different environments. This
book describes and illustrates octopuses and their behavior. The
photographs support early readers in understanding the text. The
repetition of words and phrases helps early readers learn new
words. This book also introduces early readers to subject-specific
vocabulary words, which are defined in the Words to Know section.
Early readers may need assistance to read some words and to use
the Table of Contents, Words to Know, Read More, Internet Sites,
and Index/Word List sections of the book.

Table of Contents

4

Octopuses hatch from eggs.

Octopuses have
soft bodies.

8

Octopuses can fit
into small places.

Octopuses have large eyes.

Octopuses have eight arms called tentacles.

suckers

Each tentacle has
two rows of suckers.

Suckers hold food.

Octopuses hide
from predators.

Octopuses can change
color to look like
their surroundings.

Words to Know

eye—a body part used for seeing; an octopus can move its eyes above its head and look behind itself.

hatch—to break out of an egg; female octopuses guard their eggs until the young octopuses hatch.

predator—an animal that hunts other animals; predators of octopuses include eels, sharks, and seals.

sucker—a body part that is used to stick to surfaces; octopuses use suckers to feel and to hold.

surroundings—the area around something; octopuses can change color to match their surroundings.

tentacle—a long, flexible arm of an animal; octopuses use tentacles to move, feel, and hold.

Read More

Cerullo, Mary M. *The Octopus: Phantom of the Sea.* New York: Cobblehill Books, 1997.

Hunt, James C. *Octopus and Squid.* Monterey Bay Aquarium Natural History Series. Monterey, Calif.: Monterey Bay Aquarium, 1996.

Stefoff, Rebecca. *Octopus.* Living Things. New York: Benchmark Books, 1997.

Internet Sites

About Octopuses
http://www.marinelab.sarasota.fl.us/OCTOPI.HTM

Ask Shamu: Octopus
http://www.seaworld.org/askshamu/octopus.html

The Octopus
http://www.enchantedlearning.com/subjects/invertebrates/octopus/Octopuscoloring.shtml

Index/Word List

Word Count: 47
Early-Intervention Level: 12

Editorial Credits

Martha E. Hillman, editor; Steve Christensen, cover designer and illustrator; Kimberly Danger and Sheri Gosewisch, photo researchers

Photo Credits

Chris Huss/The Wildlife Collection, 4
Craig D. Wood, 10
Dave B. Fleetham/Tom Stack & Associates, 1, 6, 12
Ed Robinson/Tom Stack & Associates, cover
Gary Milburn/Tom Stack & Associates, 16
Jay Ireland & Georgienne Bradley, 18
Ken Howard/The Wildlife Collection, 14
Randy Morse/Tom Stack & Associates, 8, 20